T0157182

habits.

habits.

JAZ EVON

HABITS.

iUniverse books may be ordered through booksellers or by contacting:

iUniverse
1663 Liberty Drive
Bloomington, IN 47403
www.iuniverse.com
844-349-9409

ISBN: 978-1-6632-1503-1 (sc)
ISBN: 978-1-6632-1504-8 (e)

Print information available on the last page.

iUniverse rev. date: 12/15/2020

I dedicate this book to the women that raised
me to use my imagination and create:
My Granny and My Mother

To the multiple creative friends that inspired me to
continue writing and creating. To the many artists, writers,
poets, and musicians that tell their stories through their craft.
Thank you for telling your story.
Because of you all, I am moved to tell mine.

Contents

Coffee. Records. Loneliness. 1

Safe. 2

Vulnerable. 3

Isolation. 4

Cope. 5

Restless. 6

Run. 7

Matter. 8

Invested. 9

Lust. 11

Pour. 12

Crazy. 13

Lights. 14

Delusional. 16

There. 17

Unknown. 18

Hurt. 20

Irrelevant. 22

Seeker. 23

Validation. 24

Open. 25

Closure. 27

Edward. 28

Silent Treatment. 29

Issues...30

Unavailable. 31

Nu Growf. (new growth).................................32

27...33

Coffee. Records. Solitude 35

It Doesn't Matter. 36

Coffee. Records. Loneliness.

I sat in my room with plenty to do. But instead I dwelled on
missing you.
And if I lost focus, I turned on a sad song to remind me that you're
not around
Although you weren't gone, you just had plans to be to yourself…
not with me
and I could've had plans too, but I chose to stay home in melancholy
playing records
Vinyls were everywhere.
On the floor, my bed, and my desk
Wish I could have more.
All of these old jams from Stevie Wonder to Donna
Summer …
but their music was too upbeat
So I put on "Single Pigeon" by Paul McCartney, "Me too. I'm a lot
like you!"
I sang loudly with my favorite coffee mug in my hand.
Pretending to be sane, so that you could notice me once again …
so co-dependent
I was dwelling on things that you would have considered minor.

Because I was not comfortable with being alone yet.

Safe.

Is it safe for me to say I'm lonely? In the middle of a crowd…
still lonely
Wonder should I leave or stay, Who would "phone me"?
I won't trip as if I think you owe me but tonight I let emotions own
me and I hate to not have control
I just want to know… who's real, who's phony?
Who would ask me where I'm at?
When I'm missing, would you miss me? When I'm this low, would
you lift me? See the bruises and the scars?
See my light dim into dark?
Would you see me? Look right through me?
Can I express my deepest thoughts?
Is it safe?
Will we be okay?
Or do you only want me when I'm great? Do you?
Do you only want me when I'm great?
I guess it's safe to say
You only play it safe
only come around to fix your plate but when the table's empty …
I never see your face.
okay.

Vulnerable.

I feel everything heavily even when it's small
No issues at all
I have trouble trying to keep a steady beat to the same songs that
everyone else owns they are in sync when they dance,
but I hold up the wall
I never really felt like I belonged
I was too this, too that
wasn't enough or always too much
If I'm not crazy, then I'm a doormat
And the problem is
None of this would mean a thing if I cared less

Isolation.

Today I indulged in something that
I've been trying to avoid
the craving became strong
I had withdrawals
I desired seclusion.

just today

Cope.

My coping skills aren't as good as they seem
I'll never live up to another person's expectations because no one can
live through me
I can only live up to who I know I'm bound to be and accept that I'm
never NOT going to mess up Then I'll get back up and fight again
because my flaws aren't the same as theirs just like my strengths
are not
we cannot be compared
I can't ask others to go easy on me
how they choose to react is their business
The only thing I know I should do is be kind and patient with myself
and allow myself to feel the pain that keeps me up at night
so that I can recover and move forward with my life

I'm not as good with coping as it may seem. I just learned to keep my
mouth shut,
Until my sorrows build up.

Restless.

Why are you always up at 3 in the morning? When the sun comes up
you can't focus
You want to be taken seriously, but are you listening to the things you
speak?
You want to be woke, you lack rest
You try to be conscientious
You say that you're blessed
And you read so much of the wrong things
Yes, you speak so well of the lies Your eyes are wide open to nothing
To get a clear view of the real
At times, you need to close your eyes
Refocus
The truth is right in front of you
It's not always that deep
Relax your mind. Sleep.

Run.

I've never been so heartbroken
Stressed
Perplexed
heaviness in my chest but my eyes are still dry
I try to cry and nothing happens
So much negative emotion trapped inside
I can't hide
feels like a dark shadow follows me around
I'm exhausted... because I'm constantly moving Quickly pacing, from
distraction to distraction When will Gravity pull me down?
When will I fall to the ground?
Anxiously fidgeting but still no weeping sounds
I'm lost ... going nowhere fast.
I used to run to music but I lost the passion and time
I used to run to a love that was never mine
I used to run to poetry that keeps slipping from my mind

And now I'm just running.

Matter.

Occupy space in my mind.
You may mean little to yourself, but don't forget,
small things can have great mass
and it's the small things that add up the most those small things can
adjust my lows
and I could walk around and act unbothered
but when I'm smiling the hardest is when I need you the most

Because you matter.

Invested.

I'm too invested
my energy, my time
Too invested
and losing my mind
You're not interested
I still listen to treacherous things and that makes my life hectic
Learning the same lesson that I should've accepted
Steps I keep missing
Trails I keep dismissing
Follow unhealthy thoughts that I should be skipping
I can help it
But the urge is so deep
I'm caught up and can't help but wonder
Would you want someone like me? if you don't I won't be shocked
because I'm a dreamer
always dreaming of someone that wants anyone
except me...
Not sure if I'm just alone or if I'm lonely Sometimes I want someone
to notice me Can you see me?
you're not imagining things
I promise, I'm silently screaming your name
Check the frequencies
You should feel me

Cause I've been sending vibes your way
Let's Vibrate.

I may have slept on you before. Please don't sleep on me. Hibernate.
I joined the party late.
But better late than never
I know this may sound strange Like how a stranger could ever be so invested...
my energy, my time.
Too invested.
Officially lost my mind. Full of resentment
Cause we haven't officially met yet...

And still...
I'm interested.

Lust.

Searching for something in you
You don't know me it's true
I've just been through some things
I should be on my knees
Praying for thanks and asking for strength
Forgive me, for feeling these things
I'm still looking for a stranger
I'm still following the danger
because I am searching for something pure in you
Perfect, imperfect you Irrational thoughts Impulsive actions
thinking of confessing my truth
I'm troubled and in love with being in lust with you.

Pour.

Want to say so much to someone I mean little to So I bottle it up and
hope it is never served to you I'll store it away
Until that day comes
To heal or reveal? I'm conflicted. What's worse?
Allow myself to feel?
Or ignore and never deal? I'll intoxicate myself
instead of getting you drunk from my burdens
But what good would it be, if my words will overflow and spill out
into your cup anyway
Neither is better than the other
Pour out?
Or pour up?
Either way, you'll feel the buzz
I'll hold myself accountable
I'll pay the fee. Drinks on me.

Crazy.

What have I done? Look what has begun
not a first, but a continuous bad impression
There's no hiding, only running but no clue of where I'm going
Something has to be wrong
Because you said something triggering
and I allowed it to get to me
I allowed myself to become irate
And when I reacted you just sat there with a smirk on your face
Oh, how well you manipulate
and how sad I feel today
I collect losses in my mind
I'm told to let it go
but I'm not sure of how to release things sometimes that affects my
faith
Yet sometimes when I lose, I also gain
I feel so much pain when you treat me this way
After I opened up and let you in
you didn't ask for it, but I thought If I did you'd find some time to burn
down your pride and in return let me inside

Why turn your back on that?
You have an obsession with not needing anyone
And I have this habit of holding on
See we both have our problems

But, I'll always be the crazy one.

Lights.

I don't take well to signals
The other passengers on a road blink their lights off and on
trying to warn me of something
What is it that they're telling me?
I'm not sure if they are signaling me or if I'm just imagining things.
My bedroom light Bathroom light Closet light
all Dimmed
And I did not heed to take action
Until they all blew out... not simultaneously
One by one
and even then
I accepted the darkness. I don't take well to hints When my phone
lit up ...
I was hoping it was you ... texting me
to check on me
And I was reminded for the 12th time this morning that I
don't have your interest
because it was not you, but just a notification from
"Pinterest"
I tried and tried to ignore my emotions
I contacted you anyway
Foolish me.

So when you gave me the signs at the time, I was so caught up
I was blind to that fact that

You will never be mine Not as a lover nor a friend This is
nothing new
Yet again, my heart sinned against me
Lead me to calamity
When will it end?

Snap out of it, All of the hints All of the signs
were loud and bright
Please don't ignore the lights.

Delusional.

Missing someone that was never present physically, emotionally
Only in my mental
Just in my daydreams
And sometimes when I'm asleep
We had nice conversations.
In my head, they seemed more intense
But when I reflect
I do regret
Allowing myself to get lost in the midst of illusions
Reading into things can cause pollution of the mind
here's a good conclusion, time to grow up
I'm the only one creating confusion
Don't know why I do this
I must escape the delusions.

There.

No place else I'd rather be. Although I wasn't invited,
I also wasn't told to leave so,
I stayed around
I was ignored at times
Yet, I was loved and appreciated ...
So you gave me some assurance, right? I decided to stick by your side
I checked in
To make sure you were okay
Or safe
I know that probably annoyed you...
I just couldn't help the fact that I cared
And I always will care
However, unfortunate events happen in this life we live in so just
know that you're always in my prayers
I hope and pray that God provides you protection
I tend to be overly cautious
And you're the kind to turn your back on fear
I promise to always have your back although I'm not near
Just lingering in the distance
But I'm afraid that someday
You might finally turn this way to see where I'm at... And I won't be
there.

Unknown.

I don't know what it's like to love someone romantically, with that
love being reciprocated
I don't know how it feels to be the star in someone's dreams
I'm unsure of what it's like to be confident in knowing
someone will always be there
I'm not very familiar with that life
So if someone asked me "you know I love you right?" I'm sorry...I
don't.
And I'm sorry to the women that were searching for
words to aid them in getting through a heartache.
I apologize that I've yet to experience a love that will encourage you
to be a great woman to a great man... I am sorry that I've yet to relate
I've only loved a boy when I was just a girl
But as a grown woman
I have not fully welcomed a man in,
because I've yet to find a man worth inviting
No matter how much I've cared for him
And when I cared, it was never mutual
And when he cared, I had already moved on.
So I'm not familiar with the love you want me to speak about
I do not have knowledge of those things

What I do know, is that I am finally trying to escape the obsession I
once had for self-sabotage
Self-hate...

I will soon be entering the double doors to confidence and peace of mind.
To the women who are on that same journey
This is for you. This is for me.
This is for us.
That is the best love to cultivate
Before welcoming a love that is unknown.

Hurt.

the drama
the extra, over the top display you portray
Girl, you better be sensitive.
I cannot imagine falling asleep each night
With a broken heart
As my favorite song plays by Ms. Keys herself
You must have forgotten that
You are in control of your emotions
Yes, you have forgotten
I still see them vividly on your sleeves
Look at me,
As I'm looking you in the eyes, because of you and I
Are one
Literally
This is your conscience speaking
Are you listening?
Don't betray me again, I have come to give you inner peace
Let's be truthful

The drama
The extra, over the top display I portray
Yes, I am sensitive
The facade, theatrics for humorous effect
But in fact, I am miserable

I can imagine waking up, dreading the next scene of my lifetime movie...

They say that I overthink, I say its anxiety

As I await a blessing to overpower this genetic "curse" I hate to say
that I'm damaged, but it's evident,
I've been hurt.

Irrelevant.

Not sure if I've been canceled
Or if I was never the plan
I've gotten way too acquainted with my feelings being tainted
Caused by flakey behavior.
And to be honest it's getting out of hand.
But I tend to replay those foul things people do
Those rude things people say Or the cares they never gave And we all
know what they say "Hurt, people, hurt people"
Well I've been hurt repeatedly and never have I lacked the
heart to intentionally make someone feel inferior
I don't understand.
And I guess that's a blessing.
Because who I am is who I've always been. Yet I'm constantly
progressing.
While others are somehow pressing
Over what?
If I don't matter...then it shouldn't matter how I talk or walk...
how I'm dressing
What it is that I'm expressing...
I can't keep holding onto others
that only want me around for superficial reasons
Status has never been a thing to me
So I'll take being irrelevant
Just like your thoughts of me.

Seeker.

What are we searching for today? What are we reaching out for?
Acceptance
Validation Attention Love
In the wrong way
From the wrong places

Are those the things you are seeking?
When there's so much more to look forward to
and someone Greater to accept, validate, and love you everywhere you
are and in the best way... from now to eternity...

As long as you uphold your loyalty.

Validation.

Lets stop holding the hands of ones that lead us to sorrow
They pull on you, let you go, and tell you not to follow
Lets stop claiming false love
Yet lets not pretend as if we have no feelings
And lets stop seeking validation from others

Just because they cover their eyes to your light, Does not mean you do not shine.

Open.

I tend to tell others that my door is always open
And it's true
Not sure if I'm willingly welcoming strangers And random neighbors
or peers passing by Or if the lock is broken
I love my privacy, but at times I can be so naive
I appear to be lost or empty
But come on in, my space is furnished and filled with the simplest yet
most precious things
some things have gone missing
Sometimes people don't respect my belongings and they take what's
not theirs
And never bring it back... like my trust and my love
But they lose sight of the fact that I have so much more
Just stored and hidden right in the back
Even so, each time I lose
It hurts me for days
Yeah, I should fix that lock, just in case
So I can secure my personal space
"Be careful of who or what you let inside." So they say
And I won't argue or disobey
Because some people take and take
Things that I would have eventually given anyway
So out of my door you crook, you thief
Others only come in to escape the storm outside
Camouflage, knowing the right things to say just to get by

Temporary resident
I know your intentions, you'll be gone by the next sunny day
You forgot something,
your wet clothes from the rain
You left muddy footsteps on my carpet because you did not take off
your shoes at the door like I asked you to. Do you see?
"I get no respect" in my own home
"I get no love" in my own space
Only because I chose to be generous to the public
No, not for any selfish gain
I never asked for a dime,
I've never asked for a thing that would put another in harm's way
My guidelines were simple and only a few followed
So only those few can stay
and to those that left on their own,
I know it's because with me, is not where they belong
That's okay.
Just know.... that someday my door will no longer be open from a
lock that's broken
There will be limits and boundaries
Despite my insecurities, I will be secure.
but if you're genuine enough with your knocking please don't give up
I just might let you back in...

Closure.

I didn't need you to fall for me
But I wanted you to care
I did not seek your sympathy
I knew you couldn't relate
I thought I'd express to you just thought I would share We don't have
to be enemies And we don't have to debate
Just because I have these feelings
And you don't feel the same So if someone is to blame It'd be my
fault
No need to point fingers
No need for exposure
Although I hate that we couldn't be closer
I'll take whatever you give
Let us close out a bad chapter.
However, my friend, our story isn't over
You've got my respect. And I've got closure.

Edward.

Those sharp objects are harmful. But they're apart of you
You never had the proper training
So you abuse others with them
I kind of pity you
But I can't stand too close to you
I cut you off before you stabbed me in the back again
see this time I foresaw what would happen
But you don't see
you're hurting yourself too
I see the scars all over your face.
Like the lies you tell when you don't get your way. But I also see the
beauty in you
You're just dangerous right now, so cut yourself free from
strangers that can't love you the way you need to be loved
Set yourself free, please walk don't run with scissors hands, this wasn't
a part of the plan But it's time to go back home.
I just pray that you let that sharp tongue loose,
I don't hate you, I forgive, and I worry about you. You know this
I hope life gets better.
Take good care ... Edward.

Silent Treatment.

We put the ignore in ignorance when we feel that it's okay
to leave someone hanging,
just to maintain our relevance.

Issues.

I hate the phrase daddy issues
My issues are my issues
Don't categorize them based on my past circumstances. Don't label
them based off of who has been in my life and raised me ...
Don't throw me in a box based on who has abused me, accused me of
anything
or assumed me to be less of the woman that I am... I said it once and
I will say it many times again...
As many times as I need to take a stance and demand the
acknowledgment of the importance of my individuality
My issues are... my issues.

Unavailable.

I heard that I keep going through things because of my availability
Somehow when I'm needed
I'm always free.
Don't make me regret my humility
I try not to forget who I'm bound to be
And who I am should not be who you think you can mistreat
I'm only wanted at your convenience
Don't mistake me for being easy
So I blow kisses to the weaker me
I shed, then grow back thicker skin This time I'm as strong as I seem
and too grown to quickly let you in
I can't control the words you cut me with
I can't control the thoughts you head is filled with
I can't count on some to refill me with the love and happiness
I once gave myself
Self-Bliss
Unapologetically selfish
When it comes to my mental health
Not saying that I'm careless
But I must take care of me too
And if that's a problem for someone else then how could we ever be cool
It can't always be about you
You were crying like I meant to hurt you

Paranoid…thinking you'll be left out
Why do you ever give in to doubt? I showed you what I'm about
Now I just want out.

Nu Growf. (new growth)

Sis,
What are you holding onto?
Those ends are split... and are damaging
Cut them... there's nothing wrong with short hair
Remember, hair grows Just like your mentality If you allow it
Trim those bad habits,
Let go of those bad friends that only want you to be miserable with them
There's nothing wrong with a small circle
You worry so much about a status
And popularity
Just as much as you want to brag about inches ... How sad
Snip snip
Trim little by little
And I guarantee you that... You will grow.
Just like your afro.

27.

Never knew I could let you go, Yet love you at the same time
I could be involved
without revolving my life around you
We could be friends Without me giving in Being your "yes man" Just
because I'm lusting Calling it "love"
Not knowing the difference
Blowing up your phone
Instead of running the ink out of my pen
I should've been writing for self-assurance instead, I was texting you,
exposing myself searching for what you couldn't give
You never did
You ignored… and I kept with the foolishness
After all this, I thought I'd never feel again
I prayed for numbness
but I realized that being numb did not mean I had strength
So I learned to keep steady
Learned to be balanced
Learned to not rely on my mind
Or my treacherous heart,
but keep myself open to the Word
And made time to rely on the Most High
What better love than the love from my Creator?

And with that love how would I ever lower my standards
I'm not looking for perfection
Who says I've been looking?

I'm focused on me ... so I don't worry about
If you, he, or she sees me
I see me.
I'm not invincible nor invisible.
And that's the love I've been craving
My Love From me To me.

Signed
- Twenty Seven

Coffee. Records. Solitude

I'm sitting in my room with plenty to do.
But I chose to relax and play a vinyl... or two. My area is spotless.
No chaos in my mind
No need to dwell on negatives... I'm yearning for a positive life...
And I'm only jamming out to anything that won't kill my vibe.
My phone is on silent and I haven't checked it all day.
I'm not sure if I was invited to anything, but if I was and
I missed the function ... I will be okay.
No pretending. No fronts.
Less time for self-hate...
I have good hot coffee in a brand new mug. And I'm having a
great day!
Because I finally know what it's like to have comfort in my own
space.
With peace of mind
I'm enjoying myself.
And I guess I have you to thank. Thank you, my friend.
Thank you Solitude.

It Doesn't Matter.

It doesn't matter where I've been Or even who I was "back then", I've made mistakes along the way And I'm stronger for it today.
It doesn't matter if I fall, I'm only human after all.
If I stumble and go back down, I have to search for solid ground.
It doesn't matter about my past, my destiny is clear at last. Once blind, but now I see.
I'm taking back my dignity.
It doesn't matter who I was before, I'm not that person anymore.
Voices of doubt can destroy, and take away all hope of joy.
It doesn't matter where I've been, or even who I was
"back then"
What matters is someway, somehow, I know where I'm going now.

- Yvonne Witherspoon

Printed in the United States
By Bookmasters